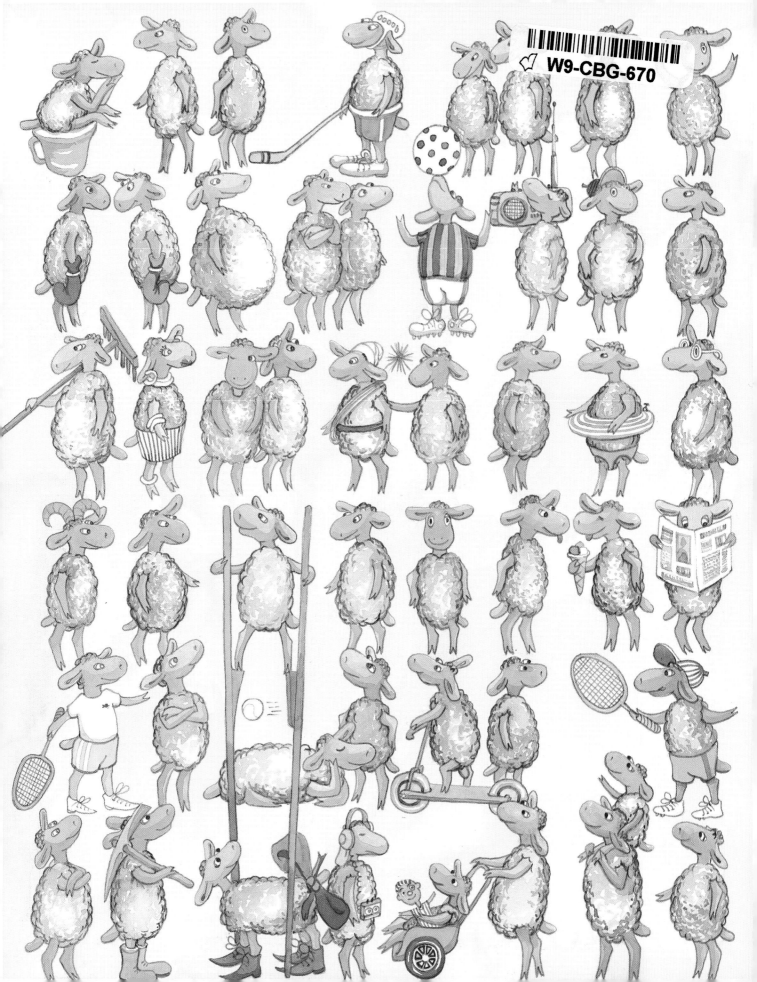

Text and illustrations by Michal Hudak.
Text of song by Annika Hudak.

The Scripture quotations are from the New Revised Standard Version Bible, Catholic edition,
© 1989 by the Division of Christian Education of the National Council of Churches of Christ in the U.S.A.
Used by permission. All rights reserved.

This book was originally published in Swedish by Verbum Förlag, Stockholm, Sweden,
under the title *Herden och de 100 fåren* © 1998 by Michal Hudak and Verbum Förlag.

1   2   3   4   5   6   7   8

Library of Congress Cataloging-in-Publication Data

Hudak, Michal.
    [Herden och de 100 fåren. English]
    The shepherd and the 100 sheep / Michal Hudak.
       p.   cm.
    Summary: A retelling of the familiar story of the Good Shepherd
who leaves his ninety-nine sheep to look for the one that is lost.
    ISBN 0-8146-2701-3 (alk. paper)
    1. Lost sheep (Parable)—Juvenile literature.   [1. Lost sheep
(Parable) 2. Parables. 3. Bible stories—N.T.] I. Title.
II. Title: Shepherd and the one hundred sheep
BT378.L6H8313 1999   98-55771
226.8'09505—dc21   CIP
                                 AC

MICHAL HUDAK

The Shepherd
and the

Sheep

A Liturgical Press Book

THE LITURGICAL PRESS
Collegeville, Minnesota

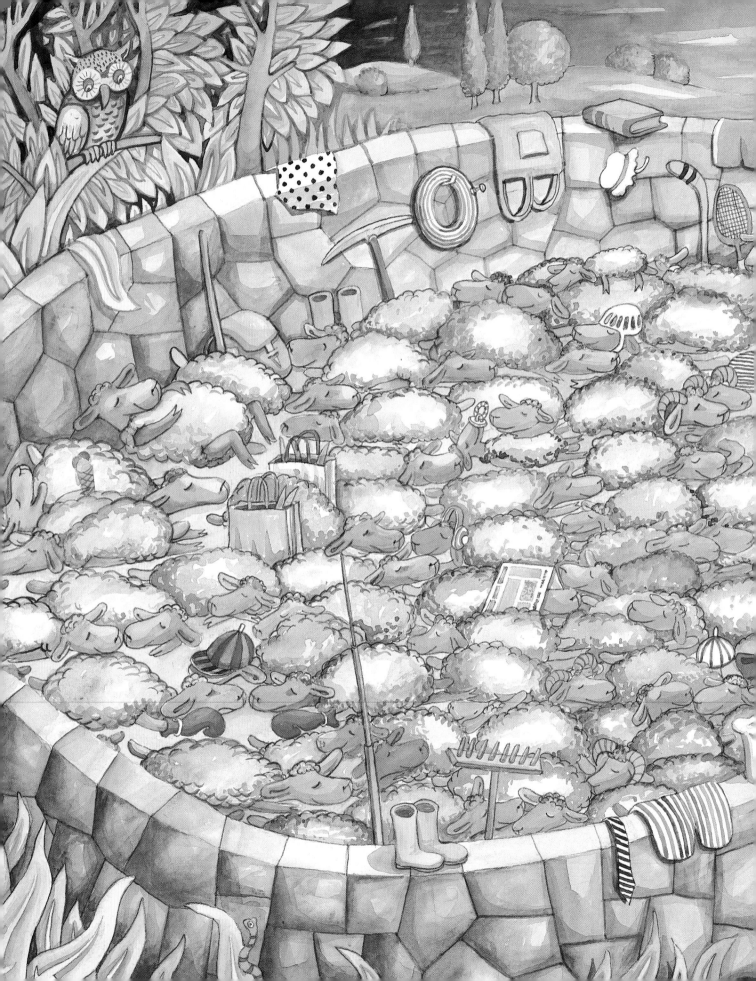

One beautiful morning little Woolly gets out of bed on the wrong side. Everything is boring—the sheepfold, his ninety-nine friends who are snoring all around him on the grass. Worst of all, he will have his wool cut off today! His coat is too thick!

"I don't want to look like a newly shorn sheep!" thinks Woolly with the black ears.

The sun has hardly risen when the shepherd stands in
the gateway and cries: "Good morning, all you sleepy-
heads! Time for grazing!" Then all the other sheep
wake up, too, and soon they are crowding by
the gate. The whole flock follows the shepherd,
jumping and skipping, and singing:

We are little animals, woolly and sweet;
we need our shepherd to guide our feet.
If he is not with us, a risk we are running
of being pursued by the wolves so cunning.
But when he is near we can live and be free;
we don't need a cage when the shepherd we see!

The countryside is barren and rocky, but the shepherd searches
far and wide and finds green grass and fresh water for his sheep.
"This is where we'll be today," he says after a while.
He sits down under a tree, takes out his flute,
and plays a tune to himself and his sheep.

Ninety-nine sheep soon find exciting things to do,
but little Woolly sits alone and does not want to join them.
Several of his friends shout to him:
"Little Woolly, come and play with us!
Little Woolly, come and play soccer with us!"

But little Woolly just mutters to himself:
"If I sit behind that bush over there, perhaps the shepherd
will forget to cut my wool today. I must go farther away."
And little Woolly wanders farther and farther away
from the others and becomes completely lost.

Little Woolly stumbles through bushes
and rocks and gets more and more
scared. All around him it is getting
darker and darker. Suddenly something
rustles in a bush. Little Woolly jumps
and starts to run as fast as he can.

Then the ground
under his feet gives
way, and he falls
into a deep gorge.

The shepherd under the tree had
stopped playing long ago and is thinking: "It's nearly time
to go home." He starts to count his sheep, but whichever way
he counts, there are just ninety-nine. "One sheep is missing. Who can
it be? Sarah is here, and Peter, and Emma, and . . . ." He knows the name
of every sheep and lamb. Soon he knows who is missing: "Little Woolly
is gone! I must find him. Wait for me here," he tells the other sheep.

The shepherd's neighbors are on their way home from their work
in the fields. "Where are you off to?" they ask the shepherd.
"Little Woolly, a small sheep with black ears, is missing," says the
shepherd. "I must find him." "Now? But it's almost dark!" they say,
shaking their heads. "You've still got ninety-nine sheep."
But the shepherd isn't listening. He walks out into the desert.

He looks in ditches and behind bushes,
and he even lifts the lid of an old well
to make sure little Woolly has not fallen
into the well. But little Woolly is nowhere.

Little Woolly is lying in thick thornbushes at the bottom of the gorge. He cannot move at all. His thick coat is entangled in twigs and thorns. Dusk sets in quickly, and everywhere he hears eerie sounds and strange footsteps in the dark. He can see gleaming eyes all around him and is terrified. The eyes come closer and closer, and little Woolly feels that a wild animal may pounce on him any minute.

Suddenly he hears a voice crying: "Little Woolly, where are you?"
"I'm here!" bleats Woolly with the black ears.
It is the shepherd who is leaning over the edge of the gorge. He sets fire
to a dry branch and climbs down to little Woolly. In the light of the fire
he can see that a cunning wolf, a shaggy bear, and a savage lion
are about ready to pounce on his little sheep and devour little Woolly.

The shepherd starts waving the burning branch,
and the sparks fly in all directions.
Soon he is fighting all three animals.

It is a long fight. At last he manages to beat the wolf and the
bear and the lion. But the shepherd is badly hurt.
He lies there beside little Woolly, without moving.

After a long while the shepherd recovers and wakes up.
He gets up slowly and cuts little Woolly clear of the bushes.
Woolly's thick coat is left in the thornbush, torn to pieces.
The shepherd doesn't say anything. He just puts little Woolly
across his shoulders and slowly sets off for home.

First the shepherd collects his ninety-nine sheep in the desert, then they all march into the village. He calls together all the people of the village and proudly announces: "I have found and rescued my little sheep. We must have a big party!" Since they are all very happy, they bring out food and drink and musical instruments. They eat and drink, play and dance, and sing:

Our shepherd is with us both night and day.
We can skip, jump, and bleat in the silliest way,
and he looks and he laughs as we skip and play.
But when darkness starts falling,
then he gathers us all in the fold.
And he whispers, "Good night."

The party lasts until late that evening!
That night little Woolly sleeps very well indeed.